BATHROOM JESUS IS REAL

BATHROOM JESUS IS REAL

P. FREDERICK

Copyright © 2021 by P. Frederick

All rights reserved. The material may not be reproduced or distributed, in whole or in part, without the prior written permission of the Author. However, reproduction and distribution, in whole or in part, by non-profit, research or educational institutions for their own use is permitted if proper credit is given, with full citation, and copyright is acknowledged. Any other reproduction or distribution, in whatever form and by whatever media, is expressly prohibited without the prior written consent of the author.

ISBN: 978-1-7336956-6-4

Library of Congress Control Number: 2021936690

All Scripture quotations, unless otherwise indicated, are taken from the Holy Bible, New International Version®, NIV®. Copyright ©1973, 1978, 1984, 2011 by Biblica, Inc.™ Used by permission of Zondervan. All rights reserved worldwide. www.zondervan.com The "NIV" and "New International Version" are trademarks registered in the United States Patent and Trademark Office by Biblica, Inc.™

Scripture quotations marked (CSB) are taken from the Christian Standard Bible®, Copyright © 2017 by Holman Bible Publishers. Used by permission. Christian Standard Bible•, and CSB® are federally registered trademarks of Holman Bible Publishers.

Scripture quotations marked (NKJV) are taken from the New King James Version®. Copyright © 1982 by Thomas Nelson. Used by permission. All rights reserved.

Front cover image from Adobe Stock
Cover layout and design by M. Gysbers

P. Frederick
P.O. Box 270413
St. Louis, MO 63127

CONTENTS

1 EXPOSED P. 3

2 A GOD THAT SEES ALL P. 21

3 SEX & SIN P. 26

4 DRUGS & ALCOHOL P. 39

5 BUSYNESS P. 43

6 CONTROL P. 47

7 THE REAL DEAL P. 51

8 PAIN IS INEVITALE P. 59

9 GOD OR BUST P. 63

10 GOD-IN-THE-BOX P. 65

11 TONGUES IN THE SHOWER P. 69

12 ACCEPTABLE ACCEPTANCE P. 71

13 DISRUPTIONS P. 73

14 KINGDOM THINKING P. 77

FINAL THOUGHT P. 81

WORKBOOK

EXPOSED P. 87

SEX & SIN P. 103

DRUGS & ALCOHOL P. 10

BUSYNESS & CONTROL P. 109

THE REAL DEAL P. 113

"Oh no! Jesus don't talk to me now. I'm on the toilet!"

"I can't talk now, God. Can't you see I'm in the shower?"

"I get my best ideas when I'm brushing my teeth. How did my mind wander there?"

These are real responses that come from real people on a daily basis. There is a belief permeating our society that teaches us that the Father of the Universe cannot, or rather should not, chat with us while we are indisposed.

This world is running nonstop. We are running nonstop. Our focus and our schedules are continuously diverted from God toward things of this world that we feel need to be fulfilled… work, school, children, sports, entertainment, travel, or daily routines such as cooking, cleaning, fixing, repairing, carpool, or preparation for the next day. Add to that the social aspect of our lives, such as parties, anniversaries, social media, family gatherings, and every other aspect of social communion. We have now created a turbine of noise that hides the peace of Jesus in our lives.

So, when the Holy Spirit, the Father, or Jesus decides to break in during your bathroom time, I would strongly suggest you sit awhile longer and find out what He's trying to convey.

Sounds strange, doesn't it? That we, as mere humans, would tell a supernatural God to back off while we put some clothing on and make ourselves more presentable. But when we think about it, how is this response any different than the response Adam and Eve had in the garden after they ate of the forbidden fruit and suddenly became aware of their nakedness?

This is a raw, real book about raw and real conversations, feelings, and fear as it pertains to the formalities and what is acceptable in our relationship and dialogues with God. After talking to hundreds of people over the years and personally enjoying my bathroom time with Jesus, I have chosen to capture some basic truths experienced by people of all ages, denominations, and backgrounds that are not often spoken about.

With all of that being said, let's begin walking down this journey of learning what it means for bathroom Jesus to be real and the significance of that chosen space of interaction.

Let's get real and let's begin…

1

EXPOSED

Genesis 3: 7-11 (CSB)

Then the eyes of both of them were opened, and they knew they were naked; so they sewed fig leaves together and made coverings for themselves. Then the man and his wife heard the sound of the Lord God walking in the garden at the time of the evening breeze, and they hid from the Lord God among the trees of the garden. So the Lord God called out to the man and said to him, "Where are you?" And he said, "I heard you in the garden, and I was afraid because I was naked, so I hid." Then he asked, "Who told you that you were naked? Did you eat from the tree that I commanded you not to eat from?"

Take a moment and think about that interaction between Adam and Eve and God. They did something that they knew God would not approve of and then they were suddenly aware of the worldly realities. It's in that worldly reality that Adam and Eve chose to participate in their shame and tried to cover up the very body that God created for them and hide from a God that cannot be hidden from. Kind of makes me laugh to consider that is what they resorted to. I mean, were they that ridiculous?

It makes for quite a funny picture if you really think about it. Adam and Eve grabbing some leaves to hide their bodies, as if God wouldn't notice the wardrobe change? Can you imagine the change in their demeanors? It had to be almost shocking to transition from all that they had and playing in the garden to, "Hey Eve, do you think God saw that?"

While we may not necessarily express the fear and shame that Adam and Eve surely felt, we often react in similar ways. To this day, we experience the same perceived "need" to cover up or push back from the exposure we are experiencing. In some ways, it's almost as if we are responding to the same shame that was felt in the garden centuries ago, as if it's an echo of the past that has been passed from one generation to another.

We don't need to run and hide, we don't need to cover up, and we don't need to wonder if He saw it. He knows all, He sees all, and still He loves us.

When God expressed His desire to connect in the garden, even after the transgression with the apple, God was lovingly conveying that He was still there. You see…when God asked Adam and Eve where they were, He knew their physical proximity. What God brought awareness to was their spiritual and relative proximity in relation to Him. He didn't ask the question for His own knowledge and wellbeing. Instead, God was lovingly pointing out, notifying, and conveying awareness to Adam and Eve of their own decision to push Him away.

Some might say, "What fools they were! They had God's full attention and they chose to let some snake distract them!"

But guess what…we do it even today.

We are tempted to be distracted, but God is always connecting…are we listening?

Imagine, the water is running, you climb into the tub or shower and close the door or curtain behind you. You let the day wash away with the soap and water as it enters the drain. You relax and listen to the sound of the water when suddenly, your mind is clear. You feel God talking to your spirit. Ideas and concepts that you had been struggling with seem to fall right into place. Perhaps you are startled with the clarity and answers to questions that had been keeping your peace at bay and you can't wait to write everything down. Your spirit soars, "Yes! Thank you Holy Spirit" jumps from your lips and you send up a high five into the invisible hand that you know was there.

Or maybe you are one of those people who has verbal conversations with God in which you speak out and feel the answers in your spirit. Ready and waiting to connect no matter when or where, even if it means in the most vulnerable places. Yes, including the bathroom.

The truth is I wrote this book as a result of several conversations I had with people who had conveyed much humiliation from "private moments" in which they felt or experienced God's presence. It was those moments when they felt so uncomfortably open and as if they were being disrespectful in feeling or sensing His presence while they were "indisposed." Embarrassment extensive enough that they shut down the spiritual pipeline until a more "suitable" or "acceptable" time. My response to hearing that was a very clear…

"Noooooooooooooooo! If God wants to chat, then God is also inviting us to listen." In other words, instead of flushing, sit for a few minutes longer and see what He has to say.

Whatever your personal story, no matter how weird it seems, bathroom Jesus is real and it's time we embrace Him more freely and put away any religious shame.

While the title of this book references the bathroom Jesus, the bathroom isn't the only place that we feel vulnerable and as a result, in many cases, we choose to make ourselves less available.

Think about that! Can you imagine telling God you don't have time for Him? I shudder to think of how it might feel if He were to tell us at different times that He didn't have time for us. I can just imagine the conversation.

Me: "Hey God, I have a question. Do you have a minute?"

God: "Sorry kiddo, a few stars got sucked into a black hole last night so I need to check on a quick fix, but we can talk later."

I mean really think about it. He's got more to deal with, and He makes time for us, but then we scooch Him aside when timing doesn't seem to work for us. Does that make sense?

Our definitions of what a relationship with a member of the trinity (Father, Son or the Holy Spirit) looks like is a real mess. He is the King; we are the servants. He is the Prince of Peace; we are the seeking. He is the connection to the spiritual realm; we are looking to learn from Him.

You see…we must come to terms with our role in the connection with the heavenly host. It's about choosing vulnerabilities with God, with intentionally making ourselves available instead of policing the what, when, and where we allow His presence to intersect with and influence our daily lives.

Here's the thing, no matter where we are or what we are doing, God's not embarrassed, and He knows when He's got us cornered or when He can make a clear impact on our time. He's a genius and He's kind of an out of the box thinker. So, it's not a matter of IF He shows up, it's when. When He shows up, we are going to be either embarrassed, hyper aware, and fearful or we are going to be welcoming. Are we willing to be welcoming to God's schedule and let Him do His own drop-in session or is it preferred that we schedule Him where we see fit?

I mean really…God knows what we are thinking about doing, so would you rather He got to you before you made a decision that might leave you with that "oh crap" moment? Or do you prefer the fun and are willing to deal with the "man, I can't believe I did that" moment? It's a real question. Some people would rather do the deed and deal with apologies later. So, take a moment and think about it. Need some more time…? Bathroom Break…

Ok, so now that you have had time to think, how about hearing that small little voice of the Lord just before or during sex with someone that is not your spouse? Have you ever heard that? That "what am I doing" moment. Or the "I promised myself I wouldn't do this anymore moment." That small pang of "nuh uh, don't do it" or the all too familiar "Lord, I'm not strong enough to say no. You're gonna have to do something here."

Ever think that the mere thought that the Lord needs to get involved so you don't slip might actually be the Lord reminding you that you're slipping? Or that what am I doing moment might actually be the Lord asking you, "What are you doing?" God may be speaking to your spirit and trying to nudge you into the straight path, all the while we are swerving like a drunk on a tricycle.

He just might be trying to get you to listen and draw you closer to that small voice rather than screaming in your ear like the devil does.

You see, the devil likes to remind you of all the things you did wrong, messed up, jacked up, said wrong, and all the times you embarrassed yourself. The devil likes to condemn you, confuse you, and give you reason to keep making that mistake over and over again. All the while, God is giving you grace to learn from that mistake, so you don't do it again.

We tend to believe the devil just enough to consider, "maybe the devil's got a point," when he tells us we are a mess and can't go to the Father of the Universe when we are all jacked up. The devil wants us to compartmentalize the Father so that He is confined to the acceptable moments in our lives. The enemy wants us to sort our thoughts between "God things versus Not God things." He wants us to be selective in what we run to God with and the things we don't, and even what God **should** be dealing with in our lives and what God **shouldn't** be dealing with.

Here's the thing, EVERYTHING in our lives concerns the Father. He's our F-A-T-H-E-R. Or if you're like me and didn't have the best earthly father role model to draw from, consider this, He's the King of the Universe. In other words, if it takes place somewhere in the universe, it concerns Him.

Man, if I could tell you all the things I've experienced and if I could tell you the stories I've been told over the decades of people having awkward moments with God. To say that God gets into some weird crevices in our lives is an understatement.

Ever deal with the Holy Spirit when drinking or doing drugs? Or felt conviction from the Father while thinking about getting high or when you've been high? If that's happened to you, you know what I mean when I say, "Talk about a buzz kill."

Why is He messing with your buzz? Because He doesn't want anything messing with His connection with you. He wants you to focus on Him, not the high. If you want an escape, then God wants to deal with the reason for the feeling of needing an escape. That's God's way of saying, "Gimme, gimme." "Gimme your hurt, release it to me. Gimme your fears and trust that I have you." God wants you to give Him that pain to deal with, give Him that mess, give Him that guilt and shame, and tell Him you don't want it anymore. Once you give it to the Father, your hands become free and He offers the opportunity for something new, fresh, and loving so you can trade up for some freedom. In other words, dump that crappy stuff at the feet of Jesus and pick up the promises of the Lord.

Here's something ironic to consider…think about all the people in our lives that we don't mind dumping on, or go out of our way to message, call, or text when we are angry or hurt. Yet reaching out to God may not hit the top ten list on what to do. Seriously, we don't mind getting on social media and blasting away at people, circumstances, and hurt, but to go to God…well (heavy sigh) hmmmm.

Here's a real deal that might twist the mind of someone who is wrestling with who God is. I heard a young lady I ministered to say it all one day when she said that heroine was her pimp and cocaine was his mistress, but God was reaching her, and she was listening. Even in her messed up state of mind, she was listening. She was answering. She didn't adopt the attitude of hope and love that God was trying to convey because the shame was greater than her hope.

Was it improper for her to talk to Him when she was coming down or fighting to stay clean? No way! It was absolutely appropriate to talk to God when she was fighting or when she was coming down. Whether or not she is able to kick the habits and adopt the truth is between her and God, but having that RELATIONSHIP (sober or not) is priceless both on this side of life and on the eternal side.

The religious thought process is that if someone is high, drunk, or unhealthy, they must not have God, God must not be in them, or they don't have a relationship with God. Oooooh this one makes me so MAD…here's the real deal. It's EXACTLY those people that Jesus came for…

Mark 2:17 (CSB)

When Jesus heard this, he told them, "It is not those who are well who need a doctor, but those who are sick. I didn't come to call the righteous, but sinners."

Matthew 9:12-13 (CSB)

Now when he heard this, he said, "It is not those who are well who need a doctor, but those who are sick. Go and learn what this means: I desire mercy and not sacrifice. For I didn't come to call the righteous, but sinners

We are ALL sinners. We are ALL sick! We just have different manifestations of our ailments, damage, hurts, and evil that has darkened our understanding of our life and our purpose. Sex, drugs, and booze are unhealthy coping mechanisms that God wants to correct with healthier and loving truths of God. He's got to meet with us somewhere, it might as well be when we are the most vulnerable.

I've seen lifelong alcoholics dump the booze after having a real come to Jesus moment before they picked up the bottle or the glass. Even when horizontal on the floor too sick from booze or drugs, some of the most powerful conversations are had with Jesus when we are at the lowest.

Ok, so it's not sex, drugs, or booze. How about those of us who are control freaks, performance mode people, or just prideful. Or maybe, God snuck in when we were in performance mode. Regardless of where we are or what is going on with us, God can and will sneak up on us without our invitation. So, how will we react? How DO we react? What are our choices saying about what we believe? What does God think about how we respond and what we are choosing over Him? Let's find out.

Whether or not we are in a comfortable place when God shows up is really of no concern to Him. God's focus is connecting with His children and conveying love, information, direction, guidance, and peace in whatever format He deems is the most effective. Fortunately or unfortunately, depending on your perspective, He's very good at His job. Perhaps too good.

But what a loving God He is to take the quiet moments or the most vulnerable moments to speak into our spirit and make His presence known. He knows at that moment He has a captive audience. He's aware that in that moment we are where He needs us to be to get our attention, and He will get it. What we do with it in that moment is up to us.

It's in those vulnerable moments that we are now focused on our response. Regardless of whether or not we suddenly become aware of our nudity or if we are on stage singing is when we are suddenly caught unaware with an image or download of information about something we are struggling with. Perhaps we're not on stage singing, but instead, the Lord decides to drop in while we're in the middle of a toast at a wedding. That seems fun, right? No, not really, but it's almost guaranteed that it will be a memorable toast for all.

Standing in the roughest parts of town, I've had many people, both male and female, walk up to our prayer team with a 40 oz. beer in one hand and a blunt in another. Sometimes they challenge us, other times we start the dialogue and ask them if they want prayer. Every time, without fail, their response makes me smile. Why? Because they often say, "You can't pray for me. I'm drunk" (or high). Do you know that most of the time when we explain to them that God knew that they were drunk and high already, even before the prayer, they look at us like we just told them something inconceivable? "What?! How do you know that?" or there is a look on their face as if they were either busted, surprised, or suddenly convicted. Most of them set down their beer and hold out their hands. Why? Because the realization that they are already seen while they are a mess, indecent, and raw sometimes gives people hope that maybe there's another option. "Well, no sense trying to hide then. If God still accepts me for prayer now when I'm wasted, then maybe he can clean me up and get me a job," was one person's response. He did all the talking to God. He was raw, open, and professed his mess.

Testimony

My ministry partner and I were in the roughest part of North St. Louis, Missouri, known for its murders and car-jackings. A man walked up, acting cool, calm, and very nonchalant. He asked for some food and some prayer. My partner and I didn't think anything about it so we both agreed. After we prayed and spoke words of truth to this man, he just stared at us. You see...he was high. He was able to communicate, but definitely high. He had asked the Lord for someone to pray with him that morning. When he left where he was sleeping the night before to get some food to tame his stomach, he was led to us. When I asked him how he was led, his response was, "I just followed the directions He gave me and here I am."

More than one person has told us this during our time on the streets. God said, God led, God moved them to us, and God let them know when we would arrive. Not one of these people were sober. There were very few moments of their existence that were not in an inebriated or altered state of mind, yet God spoke and took care of them.

How about when we are mixed up with the wrong person or people?

Ooooh man, I don't know about you, but I have a long list of people that God would not, and more than likely does not, approve of being in my life, but I allow them in because it feeds my flesh somehow. Maybe it's because of my schedule. They are available when I'm looking for someone to talk to. That works for me, even though that person is not good for me. There are sooooooooooo (eye rolling) many "relationships" in daily life that just ooze usage. People use people and then call it relationship when in fact it's ugly. Those kinds of relationships are best described as…

"Well, I'm here and you're here so I guess we are in a relationship." Neither party can come up with a reason why that shouldn't be the case, so before they know it, they give a careless shrug of the shoulders and suddenly ta-da…"Relationship."

This is where the Bible comes in handy, because there are going to be people who hang around, come around, and stay around but it doesn't mean that he or she is our person to be with. As a matter of fact, check this out…

1 Corinthians 15:33 (CSB)

Do not be deceived: "Bad company corrupts good morals."

What constitutes bad company? Bad company are those who practice ungodly thinking, do not believe that the crucifixion led to the resurrection, and those who indulge in a manner of thinking or behavior that is less than the teachings of Christ.

It's a warning label for humans! (God is funny.)

How about those other relationships that only continue to exist when one person seems to feed the pride of another? I'm sure you have seen it on television. One teen is the leader of a group and the others in the group repeat that leader's behaviors, mannerisms, and work to reflect the leaders likes and dislikes. Well, these same things occur in teen and adult relationships in the real world as well. It's funny when it's on television. It's not so funny when you wake up each morning trying to figure out who you are because you lost yourself trying to follow another.

Co-dependent relationships that seem to drone on long after they become unhealthy, become a comfortable place for many. Yet we hang on to that familiar relationship because 'we can,' rather than listening to God and letting go. God warns us again (got to love a God who provides warning labels) that we need to follow Him and not people, because people (including ourselves if we do not hold ourselves accountable) become so selfish and self-serving that the blind begins to follow the blind.

Matthew 15:13-14 (CSB)

He replied, "Every plant that my heavenly Father didn't plant will be uprooted. Leave them alone! They are blind guides. And if the blind guide the blind, both will fall into a pit."

Entitlement

Personally, I get aggravated when I'm already angry at someone and the Lord tells me I need to chill out because I'm not treating that person well. Or when I decide I'm really going to be a brat and try to justify my treatment of another and I let my anger drag on too long. Eventually, I just feel entitled to my anger. When He shows me that I'm acting like an entitled brat, I am not a fan of such information. But regardless of my displeasure at Him, God taking the time to show me that I'm being a brat is actually a merciful way of loving me back into correct footing with Him.

Regardless of what God has to say, when He pops in, He wants our time, our attention, our listening ears on, and for us to be willing to profess our mess. Not because He doesn't know, but just like in the garden, He wants us to acknowledge what we chose and to return to Him by choosing Him. Basically, God is demonstrating His open-door policy.

Regardless of when or how He pops up, He has our attention and it's time for a decision. Either engage or push Him away until we're comfortable. In that moment, we have to decide His way or our way. His timing or our timing.

It's in these times that the noise of the day is now a distant memory as we focus on what is directly in front of us. The sound of the shower, the water in the bath, the quiet of sitting alone on the toilet, the time leading up to or during a sexual encounter or standing on a stage getting into the zone and ready to perform, the mind is focused. So, it's time for God to make His omnipresence known.

How do we talk to God in the moments that we really don't feel like or want to deal with His presence? I mean He kind of just barged in the door, right? Chatting with Him was not on the agenda at that time, so now what? Here we are with a circumstance that doesn't seem to work well with the Lord in the middle of it, so now what? I'm being a bit sarcastic, but the message I'm expressing is accurate in that we often decide when it's appropriate for God to be God.

So, how DO we talk to God in those moments? With honesty and humility or with pride and control?

It seems natural for us to recoil or think that a moment of impropriety can be corrected with a perceived proper response of "not right now" while we try to get ourselves together. But in truth, it's not natural at all. Those responses are based on worldly thinking and worldly processing. Jonah did the same thing. He was not interested in God's perspective, so when he pushed back on God, God gave him an unwelcome ride inside a fish. If you don't think that was uncomfortable, then you probably haven't been fishing in a while. I guarantee you one thing, after a ride in a fish, God had Jonah's attention.

How about Moses? He's taking a stroll when a bush decides it's time to ignite. Just one bush. You know Moses had to be looking around asking himself, "Anyone else see this or is it just me?" You can bet that was an uncomfortable circumstance and God's sudden voice had to startle the man.

Oh, but wait. How about Paul walking down the road to get others to see why they need to jump on his agenda of persecuting Christians. You see, in the biblical account of Acts 9, Paul (aka Saul) is walking down a road, probably seething in his own self-righteousness, when suddenly, he hears a voice from nowhere asking why he's persecuting Him. Paul knew it was the voice of the Lord and there was no question about any of it because Paul had a couple other guys with him. They heard the voice yet didn't see anyone either. Once God confronts him, before Paul knows it, Paul is struck blind. You want to talk discomfort!? This would qualify for discomfort in my opinion.

When put in proper perspective, when God breaks in on our shower time, our toilet time, our drinking time, or any other time that seems weird, a proper response might be, "Well, I'm not in the belly of a fish, so come on in and let's chat."

One thing that is consistent in all of these scenarios is God's character. Meaning, if He REALLY has to, or needs to get our attention, He will use His authority to break through any circumstance and present Himself in the most undeniable ways. But do we want circumstances to get bad enough that He HAS to bust in to get our attention? By then, it's a pretty sure bet that we are in over our head or that we are out of order.

Ahh, but that's something else we do. We throw all the responsibility on God. "If I'm screwing up too bad, He will let me know" or "He knows how to get ahold of me."

I personally have been guilty of saying that or thinking that, and looking back, wow, I was prideful in that thinking.

But here's the kicker…when He reaches out to us and we are not paying attention, we accuse Him of not getting involved or we explain away the answered prayer and God's efforts with pragmatic cynicism.

Argh…. We are so human!

It's a good thing God both loves us and has a sense of humor because without both we would all be in a world of trouble.

So, here's a fun fact:

If we prefer God NOT interrupt us, that actually exposes the deeper issue of self-centered focus. It's an issue of a lack of commitment or a conditional commitment to the very being that chose for you to exist. It's a denial of humility and a refusal of submission. It's an exposure of our spiritual heart condition.

Ideally, we are to recall and hold fast to the words of scripture reminding us that it's supposed to be not my Will but Your Will Lord. But…we run into that human aspect of our existence and the whole understanding of sin in the world, so things tend to get a bit out of balance. It's up to us to take that time needed to think before we react and reject what God may be trying to do with us, for us, and through us. The more we know Him, the less intrusive it is and the more warm and welcoming the interactions become.

2

A GOD THAT SEES ALL

There is no hiding from this Father. I giggle as I recall old movies in which people hide behind large planters to avoid detection from others. Generally, the scene is someone avoiding being seeing by another, only to hide behind a plant or several plants, almost always standing upright with their back against the wall and trying not to move as the person they are hiding from unwittingly walks by totally oblivious. The plant hiding party breathes a sigh of relief because they got away with their dubious plot. However, God, while He may be incredibly busy, is not easily distracted by things and not fooled by the camouflage of a plant in the corner. In other words, He sees all.

Having sex outside of marriage…sees it. Drinking excessive amounts of liquor…sees it. Self-medicating…sees it.

Ever done things that you regret and hope God never finds out? Or ashamed that He has? He knows and guess what…He still loves you!!!

As His children, He's aware that some of us are brats. Maybe you're not, but I sure am. He knows that some of us like to push boundaries. He knows that some of us don't like to be told "no" or "stop." He even knows that some of us are going to know that it's Him talking to us, but we are going to ask for confirmation after confirmation until we know that we can't explain it away any further, but we are still going to have that little bit of doubt in our head that keeps us from declaring God's presence in that moment. It might even sound like, "My mind is playing tricks on me" or "This nagging thought is driving me crazy. I wish it would just go away."

He also knows that just because we are acting like brats, it doesn't mean we have ugly hearts. As a matter of fact, He loves us enough to keep pursuing us, teachings us, and showing up in places that we least expect. We are spoiled and self-centered children at times and He knows it. But here's the really strange part, not only does He know it now, He knew when we were chosen and placed on this earth that we were going to be both His problem child and His favorite prodigal child.

So why is God breaking in on our private time or the time that we have chosen to carve out for ourselves? There are several reasons:

- First and foremost, He knows what we are up to, what we are dealing with, or trying to deal with. He knows what we are struggling with, the lies of the enemy that we are toying with, and He knows how far and how fast we are beginning to trip over those lies into the proverbial ditch.
- Another reason for His barging in is because we have asked Him, "God, if you are real, then just show up." So, He's just obliging your request on His terms.
- Or sometimes we ask questions that just seem to hang out there for a while without any reply when we wanted

it, only for Him to pop up and present the answer in His time.

- Maybe you're too busy for Him during the day, so this is the only time He could get your attention without you running off the road when you are driving. Ironically, driving is when I get a lot of time with Jesus too. We kind of hang out and chat. I know He's there because I can feel Him and He knows that's my worship time, so it only makes sense that we worship together.

What we tend to do is dictate to God when, how, and where we are to get the answers to our questions, but we normally don't stop there. If we think "God doesn't talk to me" or "I want more of you God" or "I wish I had a better relationship with God, but I don't," why are we surprised with God's response by showing up?

We are all designed to hear and interact with God. He created us, He chose every cell, He chose how those cells would each be clustered, and He chose our eye color, hair color, and skin color. He chose our gifts and our talents. He chose our purpose before we entered this earth and He entrusted us with our role. Why would a God who put this much planning into our existence somehow forget to give us a lifeline in which to get instructions? He wouldn't. In fact, He gave us the one thing that no human could ever take from us. The Holy Spirit, the Spirit of Truth.

The Spirit of God, the Holy Spirit, the Spirit of Truth resides within us and receives from the Father. We have a heavenly sonar built into us. A radical point of transmission from this realm to another that no one can destroy.

How do you know that the Holy Spirit is moving within you, that you are being stirred, or that God is sending you notices that He's trying to get your attention?

What does it feel like to hear God? Contrary to popular belief, the Holy Spirit is not heard with our ears. We hear Him in our spirit. It's that feeling that catches us by surprise sometimes. Is it butterflies? Sometimes. Does it feel like electricity running through your midsection just below your ribs? Many times, yes! Is it words that just pop in your head that gives you direction, clarity, or peace? If it follows the character of the goodness of God, probably. Those are the moments when He's knocking at the door. So, what do we do?

- Do we knowingly say, "Who is it? I'm busy."
- Crack the door open just enough to verify, yep, it's Jesus, then waver back and forth as to how to proceed?
- Or do we open the door wide and say come on in?

Personally, I like to kick the door open and throw down the welcome mat, but I wasn't always so gracious with my precious time or thoughts.

SEX & SIN

Cringe worthy topics for sure, yet one that is no less real. God can and will show up when we are "misbehaving" because He's a responsible and loving Father. What constitutes misbehaving as it relates to sex? Well, the list is long. However, the most prevalent today seems to be sex outside of marriage, promiscuity, sexual innuendo, strip clubs, lap dances, seduction, group sex, pornography, lusting, wife swapping, S&M, you know…the very things that society promotes as fun and acceptable.

Here's the thing, God's watching. That cannot and will not ever change. We don't get a vote and there is no place to hide.

Think about this scene for a moment. You're in an intimate moment when all of a sudden you sense "this doesn't feel right." Perhaps your mind wanders to where you are. Perhaps it wanders to a conversation that reminds you what you're doing isn't good for another relationship. Perhaps your mind wanders to repercussions, and you quickly push them away because what is in front of you is so much better in that moment than where your mind is wandering. Staying in the fantasy that something good can come of that intimacy takes priority over the thoughts that are speaking truth. In that moment, truth is not welcome, only feeling and satisfaction. You see, it's in those annoying little moments of "this doesn't feel right" or a wandering mind that God is reminding you that you are greater than the sum of what you are doing or considering. He wants the best for us, but

He will not force His Will over ours. It's a crossroads and He's guiding the way.

So how do you respond? Do you take a moment to breathe and think? Or do you forge ahead, and the consequences be damned?

Stopping and thinking definitely slows things down like a cold shower, but it's worth it if it means hearing what the Lord, the King of the Universe, is expressing to His son or daughter about what he or she is doing. Well…it's worth it if we actually want to hear what He has to say in that moment, or we can stick to our own activities.

For those who choose to pause their activities for a moment and take a breath, it's important to remember it is hard to slow things down. Is it worth it? Yes! Why? Because it's in those moments that the creator of the very sun, moon, and stars is focused on loving us through or in spite of a choice that is actively destructive in some way.

However, the percentage of people who choose to focus on what the Holy Spirit is saying in those moments is very low. Most choose to push back the Holy Spirit, shove Jesus to the side, and check back in after the sin is complete. It's not out of the ordinary for there to be a feeling of "why did I do that?" But it's also not out of the ordinary to nonchalantly shrug it off with a "my bad, I'll do better next time" type attitude.

Maybe God is trying to get us to pivot out of those situations BEFORE it reoccurs BECAUSE He knows our weakness might be that man, or that woman. He knows that we have equated love with sexuality or intimate circumstances. Maybe He's trying to get our attention while in the moment to urge us to pull on His strength to be able to see ourselves differently in that very moment. Not to condemn, but to correct and realign us with what we are actually created for. Our purpose.

The vast majority of men and women in current American society have a tendency to indulge in sexual activity outside of marriage. I singled out American society only because that is what we currently live in and for the most part, my travel to other countries has revealed that promiscuity in other countries is not necessarily welcomed as it is here.

With that being said, sex has been minimized from something to be held in high regard and to be protected to an extra-curricular activity. I know to the younger people reading this there may be some eye rolling and a desire to close the book but hang in there. Something more is coming.

So, who are we? Are we a bag of bones, blood, tendons, and muscles with organs that have zero intelligence? Do we have to tell our heart to beat or our lungs to fill and empty? I'm going to go out on a limb and say, "Ummm, no." Unless we are on a ventilator or have a medical issue, our body pretty much takes care of the intake of necessities to keep us alive for the moment.

However, there is an intelligence within our body sending signals and information back and forth that will stimulate the necessary function from the organ pertaining to that function. What is that? Luck?

No, something greater set that into motion. Why is something greater being set into motion? Because it has a function that fits into a bigger picture that has a purpose far more extensive than any of us can comprehend. The fact that we exist is evidence that you and I have a mission and a reason for being here. That mission is to glorify the very being that gave us that function, motion, and purpose for a larger picture that will bring about forces of God that will usher in the Kingdom of heaven forever.

In doing so, the same God who created the constellations and galaxies themselves created you and I with the same attention to detail as He had when He placed every single star in its perfect spot in the sky.

You and I are masterpieces from the greatest artist ever to exist. The Father of all creation, Adonai, Yahweh, Father God, whatever we want to call Him, He is the great "I AM."

What does this have to do with sex? A lot, but religion has ruined the message.

You see, religion has used words like purity and chastity and used hell and damnation as threats for a generation (and generations to come) of rebellious children of God that have heard that story over and over again while watching some of those who are preaching it behave like heathens. For the most part, the only thing that teaching has accomplished is pushing away people with old ways of thinking, without ever explaining the real reason for the message. What's the message?

1. The message is that He loves us and wants us to have a real relationship with Him, not a shallow or even potentially counterfeit religious structure that is void of connection to Him.
2. Demons, serpents, darkness, and the Holy Spirit do not mix!
3. Rejection of God's Will for us is never a good idea.

Ok, how does having sex have anything to do with demons, serpents, and darkness?

Well, it's simple. Ask any practicing dark magic witch, Satanist, or dark magic believer and you will see that sexual practices outside of marriage are actually not only condoned but encouraged. Why would that be? As a matter of fact, those same sex practices are actually part of many ceremonies. Don't believe me? Search sex ceremonies and Satanism and ta-da…there it is. But why? Because sex introduces a spiritual exchange from one person to another and sexual promiscuity supports the worship of self.

We are made of electrical impulses. We are also very spiritual beings. We were gifted the Holy Spirit that resides in all of God's children. Some people call it a conscience, but that conscience is getting information from somewhere. Where is that located biblically speaking? In Jeremiah 31:33 and Hebrews 10:16.

Both of those scriptures say basically the same thing. That God, the creator of all things, placed His direction and His moral compass on our heart. He inscribed it so that we would not get lost in a world without a map that keeps us vectored in on what is good in a world that He knew would turn dark and cold. That, my friends, is a loving Father.

Hebrews 10:15-17

[15] The Holy Spirit also testifies to us about this. First he says:
[16] "This is the covenant I will make with them
after that time, says the Lord.
I will put my laws in their hearts,
and I will write them on their minds."
[17] Then he adds:
"Their sins and lawless acts
I will remember no more."

God's ways are not to keep us from living a full life that makes us feel good and happy. God's ways are to give us an opportunity to live a life of direction and purpose while preparing us for a place of eternal peace, health, and safety forever, with Him as our guard.

We have forgotten that God is good and has the most well-informed plan. We forget He is the five-star General of the Army and we are His army. Some of us are special ops, yet regardless of our rank, we keep trying to go Absent Without Leave (AWOL) and do what we want to make us feel better.

Adam and Eve tried that running away tactic in the Garden of Eden, but it didn't work then, and it will not work now. They wanted to do what they wanted to do. They indulged their curiosity and listened to the serpent's voice that indicated that it's not that big of a deal. They minimized their behaviors by justifying their disobedience in indicating that it's just an apple...funny, we still justify and minimize to this day. But they didn't stop there. They also accepted the lies of the enemy... Hmmmm, something we still do today as well. Oh, but wait, there's more. Adam and Eve didn't like the boundaries that were provided because they wanted to be more independent and less dependent on God...ironic, right? Wanting to be independent from the one thing we hope we never lose contact with.

Sounds crazy, right? But we do it daily to some level.

Well, it worked! Funny, we are, to this very day, trying to become individuals, independent, and fulfill our flesh with curiosities and feel-good moments.

When God asked Adam and Eve where they were, it wasn't because He did not know their location. He was asking them something far deeper. He was asking them why they chose to remove themselves from Him. Why the barrier? Why did they want more than what He was offering? Why wasn't God enough for them to fight to protect their relationship with Him? Why would they pull away? Why take the risk with sin when goodness was handed to them.

Again, nothing much has changed in how we interact with God now.

Genesis 3:9-10

⁹ But the Lord God called to the man, "Where are you?"
¹⁰ He answered, "I heard you in the garden, and I was afraid because I was naked; so I hid."

Even in the Garden, Adam and Eve were caught indisposed after they chose a way of life that God did not approve of. It wasn't the fact that they were naked that was the issue. They were naked before they ate the apple. So, what was the pivoting point? The choices they made that day.

God was fine with their nakedness. Adam and Eve were fine with their nakedness, until they chose sin, and it changed their view of their relationship with God. Suddenly, there was a perceived barrier between them and God, and it all had to do with a choice that they knew did not glorify Him, nor honor His wishes.

Now all of a sudden, when they determined they had chosen a way that did not reflect God's will, guidance, and instruction, shame came over them like a dark cloud. The way they viewed their world had now shifted. So, when they heard God's voice, they hid because they perceived they were "indecent" in the eyes of the Lord. Not much has changed since then. We have all hid at different times in our lives.

We still go through our day doing things that God may not approve of, lying, manipulating, judging wrongly, gossiping, and thinking thoughts that are not Godly, yet it's the lack of clothing that shames us?

When David had sex with Bathsheba and got her pregnant, David didn't necessarily apologize to Bathsheba, and he sure did not own up to what he did to Bathsheba's husband. Instead, David tried to cover his tracks by sending her husband to the front lines of a battle hoping that he would be killed, and he could have Bathsheba all to himself.

We do this even today, try to cover our tracks, justify, and work hard to not get caught. Rarely does it work out the way we want it to and ultimately, the sin is against God. Our sin can't be covered from the eyes of God. We cannot outrun what He sees and there is nothing that He doesn't see. So, the reality is what is the condition of our hearts at the time of our indiscretion? David's sin was tremendous and clear. Some of ours are less clear in this time and in this culture. However, the transgressions are still there. So, how do we feel when we mess up? Justified? Pompous? Entitled? God's waiting for a loving and repentant humble heart, convicted but not condemned, to approach Him with a desire to be cleansed, with a raw and revealing relationship.

Psalm 51

[1] Have mercy on me, O God,
according to your unfailing love;

according to your great compassion
blot out my transgressions.
² Wash away all my iniquity
and cleanse me from my sin.

³ For I know my transgressions,
and my sin is always before me.
⁴ Against you, you only, have I sinned
and done what is evil in your sight;
so you are right in your verdict
and justified when you judge.
⁵ Surely I was sinful at birth,
sinful from the time my mother conceived me.
⁶ Yet you desired faithfulness even in the womb;
you taught me wisdom in that secret place.

⁷ Cleanse me with hyssop, and I will be clean;
wash me, and I will be whiter than snow.
⁸ Let me hear joy and gladness;
let the bones you have crushed rejoice.
⁹ Hide your face from my sins
and blot out all my iniquity.

¹⁰ Create in me a pure heart, O God,
and renew a steadfast spirit within me.
¹¹ Do not cast me from your presence
or take your Holy Spirit from me.

¹² Restore to me the joy of your salvation
and grant me a willing spirit, to sustain me.

¹³ Then I will teach transgressors your ways,
so that sinners will turn back to you.
¹⁴ Deliver me from the guilt of bloodshed, O God,
you who are God my Savior,
and my tongue will sing of your righteousness.
¹⁵ Open my lips, Lord,
and my mouth will declare your praise.
¹⁶ You do not delight in sacrifice, or I would bring it;
you do not take pleasure in burnt offerings.
¹⁷ My sacrifice, O God, is a broken spirit;
a broken and contrite heart
you, God, will not despise.

This conversation with David and God happened millennia ago and doesn't occur anymore, right? I'm pleased to say it does occur today and will continue as long as we exist on this earth.

Yes, He's with us all the time!! (Hooray!) And yes, He's with us ALL the time. (Yikes!)

So, here's a true story as it was conveyed to me, which might make you roll your eyes for a number of reasons.

There were a couple of friends that were nothing more than friends, sitting and talking about the upcoming day. Simple topics such as what needed to be done, where each meeting of the day would be, and on what subjects or topics would be covered. With seemingly no reason, the woman stopped midsentence and said, "Hmmm, that's interesting."

The man responded with, "What?" She replied, "The Lord laid in my spirit the words 'it's time to pray,' but He did it in a feeling of a sing song voice." He smiled and considered something for a moment, but neither his eyes nor his expression gave any indication to what he was thinking. He nodded and bowed his head and began to pray out loud.

The prayer was nothing specific, just guidance for the meetings, the travel, God's Will, and for those in their lives. Once the prayer concluded, they resumed their business conversation, concluded it, and moved forward with the day's agenda. Hours went by with normal chit chat. He went and did what was on his schedule and she did what was on her schedule. At the end of the evening, each person having finished a busy day, and both were tired, He called her to recap and give her the information from the meetings she needed to put together the next day's agenda. The single question just seemed to come out of nowhere. "Can I tell you something funny?" She was more than ok with hearing something funny, but she was caught off guard by his next statement.

"Remember this morning when you said that God told you we needed to pray? Do you remember how suddenly that came to you?" He asked.

"Yeah, why?" She queried.

He went on to explain that morning when they were going over the agenda, he was dealing with lust filled thoughts and was going to begin conveying them to her.

"Oh!" she said, totally caught off guard.

He further explained it was in that exact moment he was considering what to say and how to convey it when she received the message "it's time to pray," that let him know that the loving Father saw his desires. God was proactive in giving him direction to take captive his thoughts and remind him He was watching by conveying the message to the woman. "Message received," he said to her after he explained to her what had occurred.

"So, are we good?" she asked, wondering if there was going to be any further issue. He assured her that he got the message, and it was business as usual.

Look at that love, protection, and care for His children. It was far better than a cold shower. Corrective, clear, and protective of both of them without condemnation. She had no idea, but God did. God protected him from himself and protected her from whatever may have been conveyed or acted upon, all the while protecting their relationship with God. That is LOVE IN ACTION.

It's not exclusive to this couple or biblical times. It's occurring all around us. The small voice that seems out of place and seems to make you wonder why you have an unction or direction that doesn't match the moment. Take time to determine if it is God.

Throughout my lifetime, I've heard people say, "I knew I shouldn't have done it when I was doing it, but…" Why would they know something that convicted them, but they pushed through it and did what they shouldn't have done? Because they are humans being knocked around by flesh versus spirit. We work really hard to hang onto our flesh. We love feeling good. We love feeling right. We love feeling vindicated. We love feeling the way we want to feel, but God is conveying, convicting (not condemning), and protecting us from us, if we are willing to take the time to ask, "God is that you?"

4

DRUGS & ALCOHOL

God can't talk to you when you are under the influence of drugs or alcohol, right? I can testify that this is incorrect information. God can reach us under any circumstances, period. There is nothing that can put God in a box except our belief that God can be put in a box. Here is the reality of drugs and alcohol. I have had the privilege of ministering to men and woman of all shapes, sizes, backgrounds, ethnicities, and beliefs, and in doing so, I have had some of the highest people standing in front of me telling ME about God. Prostitutes strung out on crack, excited to tell people about God. Heroin addicts going in and out of consciousness weaving back and forth trying to stay upright, reciting the scriptures, and in a full on preach. Words of wisdom and loving commitment coming out of their mouths from experiences they have had, but they were clinging to it. It was their hope.

I ministered to a woman for over a year who was a known drug addict and prostitute. She was often telling stories of people she loved to talk to about God. It wasn't in a church, and it wasn't in a mission house. It was in dark alleys, doorways that they sat in, inside the crack houses, and abandoned half burned and boarded up houses that they took refuge in from the weather. She was telling people who were high, lost, wounded, used, drunk, hopeless, and lost about the heavenly Father above and what He was doing for her, to her, with her, and through her, all the while she herself was experiencing the love of God. Her body was addicted to the drugs, but her spirit was addicted to the Father's love and connection. Her spirit was not about to let the drugs steal that connection and she hung onto the Father with all that she had in her.

Don't get me wrong, at first, she was mad when God busted in on her high and saw her at her worst, just like bathroom Jesus does when we are indisposed there, but she began to ask the question, "God, is that you?" She was excited to learn that it was. She struggled through her high and was humiliated by her condition, but God loved her through it and little by little He refined her. She was no longer a prostitute without value. She was a daughter of the King. She struggled for a number of years, but bathroom Jesus, the Jesus that shows up when we are indisposed and in a messed-up condition, slowly brought her out of that life. She's now clean, virtuous, and feels the love of the Father as a newly crowned daughter of the Kingdom of God.

If God can reach us when we are drunk and high, then what's the problem with being drunk or high? Well, there are a number of reasons but the top two on the list are:

1. God doesn't want anything to get between us and Him. He wants us to connect with Him with clarity. Think of it this way, when we get a car, we want the best speaker's, right? We want some thumping base, and we want to *feel* that music, right? We want the *experience* of that sound, right? Or when we get a television, we want the best picture and sound, right? We are always looking for some High-Definition stuff, so it's almost like what we are watching is *right in front of us and real,* right? So, why are we settling for some fuzzy interaction because of

drugs and alcohol when He's offering us clear speakers and a High-Definition experience?

He's always able to reach out to us. However, we are to create an open pathway where possible and desire to hear Him. We are always able to reach out to Him. However, when drugs and alcohol are our focus, those altered states of mind take our attention, and our connection can feel adrift from the small whisper that comes through.

The connection is relationship based. He wants us in position to respond to His unctions. He wants us to have enough relationship move according to His nudges. He wants us in position to believe in, recall the experience, and receive what He wants to give us. He wants us to have a proper understanding of what He's trying to convey. When we reject these things, reject our availabilities to Him, or try to control when and where He accesses us, a barrier or a minimization of His presence in our life is established. God is a good Father that is jealous for us. He wants our attention. He wants us to want Him more than any drug or drink. He wants us to interact with Him, but we cannot do that if we are not in control of our facilities, thoughts, actions, words, or our body. And just think, if He can reach us when we are inebriated, imagine how much better He sounds and how much more impact He can make on our lives if we are sober.

2. We are the temple of the Holy Spirit. The Spirit of Truth. When the temple is tainted with poisons, the Spirit of God can be muffled like a hand over the mouth of God. He's still there and He's still talking, but often that temple filled with filth is

like living in a house owned by a hoarder. There is trash piled everywhere but you know that there are foundational things hidden amongst the garbage and filth. You know that there is a floor. You know that there are walls. You know that there is furniture. The filth has overtaken it, but it's still there. God is still there, but the ugliness of our choices often causes us to not see Him or hear Him until we journey past the filth and seek Him.

BUSYNESS

We live in a world of constant movement and distraction. Everywhere we look, televisions, radios, computers, podcasts, cell phones, and other devices keep our attention roaming from one form of stimulation to another. Where and when does the mind have a place to settle? Take a moment and ask yourself when your mind is completely in neutral and isn't trying to produce the next thought.

It's crazy to think that maybe those inopportune moments may be the only in neutral position (receiving position) available in our lives, when we are in a place without immediate demands. I mean really take a moment and think. How many peace filled places do we have to work with?

Is your home a sanctuary of peace and without interruptions? Conversely, is your home a place of isolation, lacking peace because the loneliness presses into every memory or reminder of something lost?

Is your work, job, or office a place of kindness, cohesion, and relaxation? Does it give you the brain space to allow for free-flowing thoughts that are not restricted by the to-do list and activity around you?

Are you free of the demands of schedules and responsibilities of others? Is your life without the weight of decisions that impact others?

Our bedrooms are often filled with a spouse, children, or reminders of not having anyone, many times robbing us of peace in those thoughts or memories.

Believe it or not, the bathroom is one of the final frontiers that has yet to be bombarded with complaints, confusion, demands, or overstimulation of sound and vision. As funny as that may sound, it's actually a pretty true statement. I know many mothers that have on more than one occasion excused themselves to the restroom just to get a break from the constant demands of motherhood only to see little fingers reaching underneath the door to get closer to them. So often, moms hold back that internal scream and wonder how they can just escape for a moment. Dads are not immune to the stresses of this world either. Often, when a man can't find their way into the garage to tinker on this or that for a few moments of quiet from a crazy day at work or try to escape the demands on their shoulders that are buzzing through their minds, again, the bathroom is their throne of peace, if just for a little while. Alleyways, porches, garages, barbershops, bars, you name it, people are looking to escape. But escape to where? And is Jesus in these escapes?

In such a loud distracting world where we are continuously bombarded with information, we are under a constant assault of targeted influences and ever-increasing information. This information moves us and motivates us to remain engaged, be consumers, and focused on this world and all that this world is doing. Add to that the daily grind of work, school, errands, cooking, cleaning, and juggling the family dynamics, our brains are full.

No wonder we lay in bed thinking about all the things we didn't do, the things we did do that we shouldn't have, or the things we cannot control but we waste all of our extra time trying to solve the mystery of how we can control it.

So, where is time for God? Are we trying to get Him to fit into our existence here on earth or is our existence on earth because of God and we put Him in the center of the world and let the world revolve around that?

How can we connect with God in non-stop busyness?

- Worship music in the car is popular but having worship music playing in the background at your office or at home keeps us connected on a subconscious level.
- Look for God in daily interactions or initiate simple dialogues with Him. Just chat Him up casually.
- Take 15 minutes to read scripture OR use that 15 minutes to remind yourself what God says about you.
- If you are a dreamer, take a moment to journal all your dreams and ask Him for more information about what He's trying to convey.
- Avoid unnecessary purchases, gossip, or feel-good pursuits. (You will be surprised how much time will open up.)
- Set television limits to 60 minutes a day.

- Audio Bibles are available and are great to fall asleep to and let your mind soak in it. Most have timers, so set it for thirty minutes.
- Use workout time in the gym for audio Bibles OR trade that workout in the gym for a walk in nature. The scriptures say that God is reflected in the very nature He created. Start looking for it.

These are just a few options, but any time we take time to think about or talk to God, it's worth it.

Sometimes, when we have something that we connect with, God will use those very things to bring us closer or convey messages. If butterflies have special meaning, perhaps you have noticed that butterflies come to you in your time of grief or need. Making yourself more available for walks so that you may encounter more of what nature offers, including butterflies, might keep you further connected to the things of God.

Others find signs that pop out at them as they are driving by and receive revelation or clarity. If that's you, ask Him for confirmation. If you know that it was Him and you have peace about it, as long as it reflects the character of the Lord, thank Him for that clarity and give Him the glory in that moment.

Many notice feathers that seem to fall randomly at times of need or when looking for confirmation. Could it be God? God can do anything, so I would rather take the time to ask Him if those feathers are from Him than discredit something that was indeed a message from Him.

As long as we are connecting and reaching out to God, then God continues to build His relationship with us. – Seek, ask, knock.

Once we do this daily, suddenly there will be changes in our lives, demeanor, patience, and our priorities begin to shift. Life becomes more alive, and our character becomes more like that of the model God provided. Christ-like.

CONTROL

In case you haven't noticed yet, so much of this is about control. Lack of control, taking control, needing control, wanting control…No matter how you slice it, it's about control.

Crazy schedules and fluctuating circumstances are only part of our fight for control. We battle for control over feelings, emotions, reactions, responses, internal thoughts, beliefs, people, perceptions, and our own bodies. It's enough to make anyone scream. Because the reality is, in our desire to control so much, we have become this wrecking ball, swinging out of control. All that we really need is God to step in so we can rest, but we need to move out of His way and let Him do what He needs to do.

Have you noticed that these hectic schedules often begin and end our day without any real input from what our body or minds really need?

We can find ourselves mindlessly checking box after box, meeting after meeting, appointment after appointment, running errand after errand, with no real break. We find ourselves exhausted, frustrated, and aggravated. Kids, lack of money, pursuit of money, housing issues, friend issues, family issues, life just spins and spins and spins! Why? Because we are out of control.

Oh, then it gets even weirder. We find ourselves trying to control the **lack of control,** so that things don't get "too out of hand." It's ludicrous to think this is the way we are meant to live, yet we keep trying to do it.

What's even more impossible is we are in the mode of trying to control our life or control the lack of control so that it doesn't get more out of control, all the while telling ourselves that we are submitting to God. What are we thinking?! If it weren't so serious, it would be funny.

We somehow think that we can control our daily life or control the gradual slide from lack of control to some extent, and yet still submit our daily life to God at the same time. How exactly does that work?

God doesn't just work in our prayer time; He's working in our daily life as well. So, if we are truly submitting to Him, why are we white knuckling our day?

It's like trying to chase down and bottle up the wind! Just stop for a moment and BREATHE! Get off the hamster wheel of life and just sit down with Jesus.

God has a plan that's better formed than our own, so why don't we just let God do it His way?

> Proverbs 19:21 (CSB)
>
> Many plans are in a person's heart,
>
> but the Lord's decree will prevail.

You see, the more we try to control the more out of control we actually find ourselves to be. It's in that place of being outside of control that we find ourselves in a position to accept God's presence in our lives or push Him away and keep fighting for control. We have options:

- Ask for help from people and peers that you trust and live according to Christ.
- Go to God in raw real prayers and don't be afraid to show true emotions when talking to Him. He already knows what's going on inside of you, letting it out is a release that He can work with.
- Look for the blessings in the parts of your life that you did not or could not have planned.
- Be purposeful in your choice to allow nonessentials to slip through your grip and let God show you another way.
- Find some time to just be quiet. Read. Walk. Just stare at the clouds in the sky…just find little bits of quiet.
- Express gratitude to God regardless of the circumstances by recognizing no matter how bad something appears, it could always be worse.
- Recognize the privilege that you are still able to love and be loved by Him.
- Put healthy boundaries around social media, television, and technology so you can take time for God.
- Look outside yourself and see the circumstances of others that are less fortunate than yourself and discern what you can learn from that.
- And if God is nudging you to assist in helping a ministry, feed, donate, or volunteer, regardless of schedules, perhaps giving it a try might change some perspectives.

Let God's plan prevail because it's going to anyway. We just keep swinging at the wind, but God moves in the wind. Breathe…

Pick two of the above bullet points and do those for three weeks, then reassess yourself and reassess your connection with God. Learn yourself because God already knows you…and He LOVES you.

THE REAL DEAL

What is acceptable in our relationship with God? Ooooh, let me tell you there is a long list of reasons people feel they can't talk to God.

I'm mad!

I'm a mess.

I can't take any more.

I just don't care anymore.

I'm at the end of my rope.

Well, He let me get into this mess, why would I go back to Him.

He can't see me anymore.

He can't hear me anymore.

I can't feel Him anymore.

I've never had a connection with Him.

I'm embarrassed (ashamed) at what I've done.

"I'm good," "I'm fine," or "He already knows, so why do I need to say it?"

I pray at night and it's daytime now, so…

I'm busy. I have kids, a job, and a crazy schedule. I don't have time to take a shower, let alone time for prayer!

He let this happen to me.

He didn't stop it, but He could have, so why would I talk to Him?

I'm not good enough for God.

I can't pray because I'm going to yell and scream.

And there are SO many more. Here's the thing, this is when we are to talk to Him, but because we think the way we think, He has to do a sneak attack to get our attention.

Religion has taught us that proper prayer must look and feel a certain way. It must be quiet, fold your hands, speak softly, have the right words, don't be rude, and don't raise your voice. But our Father in heaven already knows our struggles, our thoughts, and our fears before we do. We are not hiding anything no matter how hard we might try. God's not passively checking in on and observing humanity in between other priorities. We are a priority to Him. We are His children.

He knows that little Sally hasn't checked in for a while, but He isn't indifferent in His awareness of Sally's absence, and He isn't shying away from the hard or uncomfortable dialogues with thoughts like, "Well, she was kind of snippy in her prayer the other day. Maybe when she's feeling more herself, we can chat."

Our Father, Our God, Our King of Kings sees Sally struggling in her heart. He sees the pain. He sees the exhaustion in her eyes. He sees the betrayal that was done, and He sees the hopelessness regardless of how long-term or short-lived it may be.

So, can we talk to God when we are angry, sad, ashamed, or experiencing any other feeling or emotion? Yes. He wants that and He won't yell back. He will love us and love you through it.

Where do you start? Open your mouth and just say something. If you want a relationship with God and you are angry at Him or what was done to you, then let it out and yell. Just start talking to Him. The first step is to open your mouth and say something to Him.

It can look like, "God look, I don't know what your deal is, but I'm really pissed at you right now."

There are those in the religious sectors of church that teach and believe that such a conversation is blasphemous, sacrilegious, or even disrespectful. That's ridiculous. You are His child. He knows your heart and the reason behind your outburst. Being angry at God is not unrealistic, it just means we are still working on wisdom. And just like children, we don't always know how to say what we are crying and often screaming inside to convey, so we spout off. How do we know when we crossed the line?

When we stop going to God for help, guidance, and hope, and instead start speaking anger or hatred to Him. When we choose evil over hope and life. When we choose to turn away from salvation and choose damnation.

You see…we cross the line when we let anger drive away our faith. God can get through any emotion we have, as long as there is a seed of faith.

David cried out to God in pain, sorrow, anger, and even questioned God and He was a man after God's own heart.

Psalm 42:9-10 (CSB)

I will say to God, my rock,
"Why have you forgotten me?
Why must I go about in sorrow
because of the enemy's oppression?"
My adversaries taunt me,
as if crushing my bones,
while all day long they say to me,
"Where is your God?"

Our Lord and Savior is looking for a relationship that allows us to connect so we can grow closer to Him. Reverence comes with a loving understanding of His goodness, loyalty, and a healthy fear of never getting a chance to abide with Him in eternity.

I know, I know, eternity is too huge for many to even process, so we often just gloss over it as a word that means forever. What is forever and how do we wrap our thoughts around that, let alone fully understand the magnitude of it.

Let's talk about that for a quick minute. Think about the sky for a moment. Have you ever taken a moment to look into the depths of the clouds and the stars and wonder what is beyond? We hear what those who have traveled outside our atmosphere have said. We see what the cameras have captured, but does it feel real to us here with our feet on the ground? The fact that we have not personally experienced it doesn't make it any less true. If we were to go even further with that concept, consider the photographs and videos we have seen, in which our universe seems to go forever, and it takes thousands of years to get from one planet to another. What if eternity was even that big? Would that be impressive enough? For me, it would be, but God is bigger than that, so eternity goes beyond exponentially. So, if we had a potential opportunity to sit in a garden of peace and beauty, surrounded by love and no more pain for at least a thousand years, would it be worth it? I don't know about you, but I could sure use that break in my life.

A chance to hang onto and hang out with God in peace for a couple thousand years. Yup! Sign me up.

I don't need to know the extent of what eternity means; I just need to know that it's an option. I also need to decide if I'm willing to settle for a temporary "feel good" in chasing social media, good food, money, nice cars, sharp looking clothes, and other feel-good stuff that only makes me feel good for a while.

Or if that thousand years of peace and hanging out with God is going to get my attention long enough for me to really check it out. The most important investment we will ever make is in our relationship with God. Let's run after what we were created for and go to the creator himself to help Him teach us who we are.

Colossians 3:9-17 (NKJV)

9 Do not lie to one another, since you have put off the old man with his deeds, 10 and have put on the **new man** who is renewed in knowledge according to the image of Him who created him, 11 where there is neither Greek nor Jew, circumcised nor uncircumcised, barbarian, Scythian, slave nor free, but Christ is all and in all.

12 Therefore, as the elect of God, holy and beloved, put on tender mercies, kindness, humility, meekness, longsuffering; 13 bearing with one another, and forgiving one another, if anyone has a complaint against another; even as Christ forgave you, so you also must do. 14 But above all these things put on love, which is the bond of perfection. 15 And let the peace of God rule in your hearts, to which also you were called in one body; and be thankful. 16 Let the word of Christ dwell in you richly in all wisdom, teaching and admonishing one another in psalms and hymns and spiritual songs, singing with grace in your hearts to the Lord. 17 And whatever you do in word or deed, do all in the name of the Lord Jesus, giving thanks to God the Father through Him.

How do we help Him, you ask? Good question. By taking time to listen, abide, and receive.

What generally happens is we let pride start running our agendas. We start to think if life doesn't look like we want it to, if the journey doesn't feel like we want it to, and if the turnaround of the results aren't quick enough, then why bother pursuing it.

That is pride, control, fear, and often past pain of disappointments that are coming to the surface. It's easier to not trust in something than to get our hopes up in something that may never be proven, true, or come to fruition. That's pride.

Here's the thing, pride didn't work out really well for Lucifer, so we have an idea of how all that turns out. For a quick recap on Lucifer, he was close to God, helping and overseeing various aspects of that realm. Lucifer was created to be gorgeous, in charge of music in heaven, and surrounded by jewels and gems. He was powerful and with authority, but that wasn't enough. Lucifer got cocky and wanted more than what he had. He wanted God's seat and rebelled until he was thrown down and ejected into the earth. You see, God didn't accept that kind of attitude from the angel of light. Lucifer was lost because of His pride.

Does that mean if we are prideful, we will be lost too? No, not necessarily. We have had the privilege of Jesus coming to release us from that snare.

So, Lucifer got cocky and prideful and was cast out. Adam and Eve got cocky, prideful, and decided that they wanted to do things their way and that didn't work out. Why do we keep trying the same routines knowing it doesn't work out in our favor?

One answer is because the "old man," the unfinished self, is still in charge and our "new man," the sanctified self, has not yet matured.

And because Sin entered the earth and now, we are faced with hard decisions every day. God's way or our way.

What does God want from us? God is looking for humility, humble and willing hearts that are seeking peace, truth, and love. His arms are open, and He loves us enough to bust in on our bathroom time to remind us that He's here, He's with us, and He loves us.

When pride dictates our relationship with God, we find ourselves on the losing end of that deal. Why would we set ourselves up for loss when we spend a lifetime trying to get ahead? He has more information than we do, and He knows the end from the beginning, so how can we lower God and His decisions to fit our expectations for outcomes?

Isaiah 55:8-9

"For my thoughts are not your thoughts,
neither are your ways my ways,"
declares the Lord.
"As the heavens are higher than the earth,
so are my ways higher than your ways
and my thoughts than your thoughts.

PAIN IS INEVITABLE

One of the reasons we try and control our relationship with God is out of pain. First of all, anyone who has not experienced pain hasn't ventured out into the world or been on this earth very long. Everyone, including myself, has experienced pain in varying degrees. If you are one of the fortunate people who haven't had anything occur of any real consequence, you are very unique. I'm not going to do what many teachers, preachers, or authors do and write that we were warned, and we would have pain in this world. Albeit true, I'm not going to go down that road.

This is a plain old raw everyday let's deal with daily reality conversation. It's not popular to think that we need pain, discomfort, and loss to grow in our faith, but it's true. I'm not speaking from some flowery place of "God is good, so roll with it" position. I'm coming from a position of "Yes, God is good and perfect, but life is rough and painful, so what do I do with this pain?" The ultimate answer is give it to Jesus and let Him deal with it so we can start over or begin to move forward, but how do we do that when we don't know how to get past the ditch we are in?

I have had much pain in my life. Throughout my life, if I were to take inventory of what I have risen victoriously from, it would include being raped daily for years, beaten for years, looked down the barrel of more than one gun as they were pulled on me, knives cutting my flesh in an effort to control what I say and do, best friend murdered, nieces that died before I got to know them, divorced, abandoned, so many losses from people who graduated into the kingdom far too early, and betrayed too many times to count. These are just a few of the pains in my life I have had to process in the last fifty years.

In each of those, I suffered. I cried. I screamed. I cussed. I grieved. I got angry. But the one thing I never did, was surrender my connection to the Heavenly Father to the enemy. That was mine. No one could take it from me. It was mine. No one could tell me it wasn't. It was MINE to hold, protect, and remember. It was MINE to be raw with and when I was at my loneliest moments, I knew I wasn't alone. When I was at my lowest, I knew He was standing guard and reaching His hand to lift me up. When I was my angriest, I knew He was sitting there waiting for me to crawl into His lap.

It's through those moments that I became so sure of His desire to love me, protect me, defend me, comfort me, and lift me up that I transcended the circumstances, transcended the pain, transcended the anger, transcended the flesh, and found forgiveness and let go of what I thought I could control or the anger of what I couldn't control and said, "Enough!"

I would no longer fight the memories. Instead, I looked past them to see what God has done with me since then. How God used those things that occurred for His sanctification of me, for where He was able to take me, for how I can now walk and talk a different language that is real to the people who need to hear it. I have TESTIMONY that draws me from the inward facing memories of what was done to me, and He moved it outward to convey hope and proof of what He WILL do as we move THROUGH the mess.

Had I let my circumstances or pride dictate my relationship with God, I may have sat with my anger, my schedule, and what I felt it should look like. In doing so, I would have lost time with the peace, love, and connection that He gave me when I chose to trust Him. Instead of fighting for my trash T.V. nights or my guilty pleasure shows, I put my effort in sitting with my Bible and reading. Now, during my moments of indiscretion, I include a welcome mat for the Lord to pop in and maintain a teachable spirit for when He would like to chat.

GOD OR BUST

We have entered a time when we need God more than anything else. The reality of this world is a reflection of what is occurring in the spiritual realm. There are more than profane words and lack of morals and ethics going on in the spiritual realm. However, we are all affected. We are dealing with principalities and powers that influence our world.

Ephesians 6:12

For our struggle is not against flesh and blood, but against the rulers, against the authorities, against the powers of this dark world and against the spiritual forces of evil in the heavenly realms.

Our murder rates are rising. What used to be right is now wrong and what was condemned by God is now condoned by society. We are upside down and we need God to keep us from sliding into this world even further.

It's time we celebrate the surprise visits of Jesus no matter where we are or what we are doing. Calling on Him is only part of the equation. Expecting and trusting that He's already there, listening, believing, surrendering, and letting Him take the reins are the rest of the equation.

God loves us, so He will interrupt our plans like Jonah.

He will interrupt our sleep, our nap time, or even our moments of quiet.

1 Samuel 3:9-10

So Eli told Samuel, "Go and lie down, and if he calls you, say, 'Speak, Lord, for your servant is listening.'" So Samuel went and lay down in his place.

The Lord came and stood there, calling as at the other times, "Samuel! Samuel!"

Then Samuel said, "Speak, for your servant is listening."

He will even send a representative from Heaven to make sure contact is made and information is conveyed to guide, protect, or warn.

1 Kings 19:5

Then he lay down under the bush and fell asleep.

All at once an angel touched him and said, "Get up and eat."

GOD-IN-THE-BOX

Have you ever noticed when suddenly someone you have not talked to in a while just pops into your head? What do you do with that? Where did it come from?

Do you push it away as wasted energy and turn up the radio or keep going on about your day without another thought about it?

Here's the thing…what if God is trying to reach you to ask you to pray for them?

Did you ever notice that sometimes after you mention someone's name, they suddenly call? Coincidence?

What if there was a spirit-to-spirit connection giving you notice that someone was thinking of you?

What if it was a warning to help you avoid that person or place that they frequent?

When we put God in a box, we are limiting the information that He is conveying to a logic that does not apply to an omnipresent, omniscient, perfect, and sovereign God.

God does all these things. He warns. He asks you to pray. He connects you to others. Why minimize any of those things as coincidence? How does that glorify God and what benefit is it to you to push it all aside?

I remember a time in my life when there was a man that was not good for me. He was out one evening and I was folding laundry.

I without a doubt felt the moment he was with another woman. God didn't warn me to hurt me. He warned me to protect me. That evening, I confronted the woman and she confirmed they were together that evening for the first time. That was the end of that.

Just this morning as I write this, a woman's name kept coming to my mind. I reached out to her via social media, and she was just thinking of me that very morning. We were each struggling with some daily stresses in our lives and were just soldiering through it…alone. But God put us together and together everything felt lighter.

What does pushing back the Lord do to benefit us in any way other than feeding the flesh? The very flesh that the scriptures warn us against following, causes us to miss the things that He has planned for us, or delay the blessings that are waiting.

What we do as a whole, is live our lives based on what we perceive we want, we need, or we have to do and then ask the Lord to Bless it.

Listen…if that's what we want to do, God will let us run with that for a while, but when we go crying or praying to Him about why this or that isn't going right in our lives, don't be surprised when He reminds us that we didn't ask Him first before jumping head long into those circumstances.

Parameters

"God, he's a good guy," or "She's a good woman. Bless this relationship."

"God, you know how badly I want this trip. Send me the money for it."

"God, you know I want this house. Find me a way to get it please, in the name of Jesus."

"I know you want what's good for me and you want to prosper me, so I believe you are sending money my way."

"Lord, you know I need a new car, but make it a nice one, Mercedes or something. You don't do anything small, so do it up right Lord."

God is not our personal genie in a bottle. I don't care how many times you rub that bottle you have, God is not going to jump out of it and say, "How may I serve you," or "You get three wishes…go."

And who wants a God that even thinks like we do. I sure don't. I want someone bigger, smarter, more powerful, that sees beyond where I am at, and knows where I'm going. So why would I put parameters around God's actions with me that serve me when I don't know what I'm doing?

None of us know what we are doing. We are just flying by the seat of our pants trying to make it through this jacked up ever darkening world and keep our heads on straight long enough to make it to the end of our life journey. So why would we dictate what God wants us to have?

Nope, that is above my paygrade, and I can safely say that's a job I will never sign up for. Letting God be God is the only way for any of us to become who we were intended to be.

11

TONGUES IN THE SHOWER

So…funny story. True, but still funny.

As a small child, we were pretty straightforward Christians. Church on Sundays, prayers at dinner, and the traditional "Now I lay me down to sleep" type prayers before bed that seemed to have existed long before me.

When I was a teenager, I found myself doing what I normally did seeking a safe haven from all school pressures, the bullies, and the teenage dramas. I was in the bathtub listening to the water and saying my prayers to my heavenly Father. I loved praying. It was truly a sanctuary for me.

I pray silently at times. I pray out loud when I want or wanted to declare something, get emotional about something, or when I praise Him. But on that faithful day, I was stunned as gibberish came out of my mouth.

It was a normal prayer in English. I said my prayers, made my immature teenage requests, and I began praising the Holy Father and declaring how much I loved him (and still do).

Without warning, my English prayer became this gibberish. I stopped in shock. I started to speak again, and again, more gibberish. I got scared and began repenting over and over again as a scared kid does. I still remember the fear that I had done something wrong. I still remember the "I'm sorry God. I don't know what I said. If it was bad, please forgive me. If the devil got ahold of my tongue, please forgive me and protect me."

Looking back at that moment as an adult, I just smile. I giggle as I think how silly it was that I was scared that the devil had gotten ahold of my tongue and somehow, I had insulted God. I was so immature in the spirit and so uninformed as a straightforward, tow-the-line taught Christian. I had no idea that what happened to me was miraculous. I had never heard of being baptized in the Holy Spirit, and I sure didn't know that it could happen the way it did!

I recall feeling so badly about it that I got out of the bathtub, wrapped a towel around me, and cried as I sat on the floor. I thought about asking my mother, but as soon as the thought came to mind, the shame of what I thought I did wrong was just too great for me to vocalize.

Now, as an adult, I understand what took place. The Lord met me when I didn't know I needed to be met with. He was loving me when I was loving him.

ACCEPTABLE ACCEPTANCE

So, what is acceptable exposure to the Father and what is acceptable exposure to you?

Jesus was mortified in front of the world for us. Us, not just our forefathers, not just our ancestors, but us in today's world. What Jesus did for us on the cross removed more than just the veil, it reached backward into time and reached forward into the future. We received the privilege of being included in something we were not even there to see, but we still get to receive the inheritance of that moment.

The Lord created a pathway that removed eternal death from the grave and introduced eternal life. If the Lord is willing to go to those lengths to cover us so that we can return to him by absorbing all of our sin, all of our shame, and all of our filth, then who are we to determine when and where God wants to reach us? Our Father, who art in heaven, hallowed be thy name. Hallowed...Think of that. His name is hallowed. This means holy, revered, respected...who are we to dictate our relationship with an entity that took such careful time to pick every wonderful and good thing about you. Your eyes, your skin tone, your heart, every cell in your body, every hair on your head, every tooth in your mouth, and He called you His.

Before we entered this earth, He encoded a mission and guidance within us. And just like His son Jesus, He assigned a purpose to our existence before we took our first breath. (Sigh...)

Bathroom Jesus is Real

God is one amazingly cool cat to put up with all of our mess and still be willing to hang around, love us through it, and even give us hope and promises of His loving acceptance "in spite" of ourselves.

DISRUPTIONS

Let's talk disruptions. A topic that can be cringe worthy for those who either experienced it or for those who are in it.

We have lots of ideas and plans for our day, our week, and even our lives. We think we know what we want it to look like and once we determine what that is, we run after it until that vision becomes our reality. Or at least we try.

(Pause for sarcasm warning that begins in 3…2…1…)

Because we know what's right for ourselves, right? We know what's best for us, right? We have all the answers, right?

Let's take a moment to stop being so superior for just a quick moment and go to the book of timeless answers.

Proverbs 19:21

Many are the plans in a person's heart, but it is the Lord's purpose that prevails.

In all seriousness, we have such great intentions or so we think. Ultimately, the reality is most of our plans focus on what we think and what we feel, instead of what God conveys or where or how he urges us to move. In other words, we like to feed the flesh. It's the beast that seems to be insatiable. The beast of flesh wants to rest when God says move. The beast wants to eat when

God says fast. The beast wants to lust when God wants to remind us that those thoughts are not of Him. The beast wants to look the best, smell the best, drive the best, live in the best, and be the best, but the Lord just wants us to show up, be present, stay in tune, and walk forward into our purposes.

Remember the story of the Tower of Babel in the Bible? They had an agenda. They had this brilliant idea of building a tower that would send a message of power, control, and equality to everyone, including the Lord (Genesis 11:1-9). God knew that they were about to get too big for their britches and needed a bit of an attitude adjustment. Why might you ask?

They had gotten such an ego boost going that they were soon going to become independent from God and turn their back on His position in their lives.

What's God going to do…just let that kind of pretentious pompous pride go unchecked? Nope. God determined that they were too focused on themselves, and they were beginning to act like ungrateful rebellious gang members trying to take His territory. What they didn't know was God was letting them only go so far with their plan before He bust up the gang. He changed everyone's language from one that everyone could use to individual languages that created barriers and scattered them so they couldn't regroup. If they were going to come against God and challenge His authority, He was going to make them work harder for it and give them some time to rethink their agenda.

That's what a good Father does. Gives us a little reminder that we don't know what we are doing as well as He does, even when we think we do. In this case, He just gave them a supernatural timeout, so they had some time to think about their choices. That's mercy.

Changing their language to other languages is quite an attention getter, but it's not the only one God used and He's still using attention getters today.

If you are in the very beginning of recognizing that God is actively changing your plans, hang on, it may feel rough and maybe a little unfair, but God's plan is so much bigger. Some of the biggest changes come when our lives get shaken the most. It's painful at times, but most growth requires it. If it was without pain, how would you know that you grew? God doesn't inflict the pain, we do it to ourselves with our own resistance. Sometimes, others inflict the pain and God has to walk us through it, but God is always about movement.

If you are in the middle of God disrupting your plans as we speak, in all sincerity, I say, "Congratulations." God is actively engaging you in His plans, Kingdom plans, and He's moving you toward something that perhaps you would not have moved yourself into or toward at this time in your life. You may not see the purpose at this time. You may not even understand how you are feeling about it, but something is occurring, something is changing, and something is progressing or even traversing the unseen.

Then there are those who are watching the chapter close on the changes that were made in their lives. They can see the testimonies that came from it. They can see the growth and the new directions that are now opened to them that were not visible to them before. To those I say, "Welcome." If that's you, then you are staring at something that seems to be unwritten and vague for your future, but I promise you it is known, written, and designed for you to move into. You may be that person that makes a change in someone else's life. You may be that person that suddenly finds your life redefined. You may be that person that just finds peace in the storm so that others may see God in you. You may be the healthier version of you so that you may sow love and laughter into children and teach them about the Lord and what He did for you. You may have a role that others build off of. Whatever it is, welcome to Kingdom thinking.

KINGDOM THINKING

Kingdom thinking is understanding that what is in front of you, your circumstances, your feelings, your situation, is not necessarily what it may seem.

Kingdom thinking not only recognizes that there are unseen forces at work, but also that we have authority that flows from the throne of God through us that influences every circumstance, situation, and impossible hurdle in our lives. We are His children, and we are taken care of.

You see, what is occurring in the flesh is normally a direct reflection or a result of what is occurring in the spiritual realm. Almost like a mirroring affect.

An example might look like someone with anger issues. However, that may be just the physical manifestations of a trauma that occurred long ago. On the spiritual side, that person may be reliving something that is tormenting them, and their only known outlet is anger. So, something tormenting (ungodly) becomes manifest in the flesh as anger. It's in those ungodly moments, those dark moments, that torment enters and can change something in how we process information and how we respond. Remember, we are not dealing with flesh and bone my friends. We are dealing with principalities and powers. It was only in recent generations that spiritual matters have been minimized or even pushed out of consideration, as scientific methods of thinking and explanation have taken center stage.

We must keep the spiritual realm within our thought processes when considering what may be occurring in us, with us, and around us.

Ephesians 6:12

For our struggle is not against flesh and blood, but against the rulers, against the authorities, against the powers of this dark world and against the spiritual forces of evil in the heavenly realms.

Perhaps your circumstances around you lead you to feel as if you are living in squalor or low income. However, what if you are in position to reach people on a level and in a place where others are not designed to be. What if you are not living low income but instead, you are living in purpose? Some might say that's not fair. How come others get to have more? Live more comfortably? The answer may not seem fair, but it may be that you are in position to reap something more in heaven.

Luke 16:22-25

The time came when the beggar died and the angels carried him to Abraham's side. The rich man also died and was buried. In Hades, where he was in torment, he looked up and saw Abraham far away, with Lazarus by his side. So he called to him, 'Father Abraham, have pity on me and send Lazarus to dip the tip of his finger in water and cool my tongue, because I am in agony in this fire.' "But Abraham replied, 'Son, remember that in your lifetime you received your good things, while Lazarus received bad things, but now he is comforted here and you are in agony.

In other words, having all the things that give us comfort, status, and treasure here on earth may nullify the treasures we reap in heaven. The story of the beggar named Lazarus and the rich man is best explained like this. When the beggar died, his lacking in status, lacking comfort, and suffering here on earth was acknowledged in heaven, but also what was acknowledged was Lazarus' heart. The rich man got all the comforts, status, and had a life of riches which probably came with power or perceived power and control. Once both the rich man and the beggar died, it was the rich man that now needed the poor man to comfort him. The poor man got his riches in heaven while the rich man was pretty much tapped out.

There are many scriptures that explain such things as this. Matthew 19 and Luke 18, as well as:

Mark 10:25

It is easier for a camel to go through the eye of a needle than for someone who is rich to enter the kingdom of God.

As well as the story of the young rich man in Mark 10:17-31.

Here's the thing…we can choose our agendas here on earth. We can chase our perceived desired outcome and we can pray for and pursue things that feed our flesh or things we feel entitled to, but personally, I'll wait until Jesus determines what I am to have on this side of my journey, and I will accept what He has waiting for me on the other side of the journey. Because there is one thing I do know about myself, if I plan it, if I chase it, if I desire it, it will probably take me more into self than that of God. I like my food too much and my body reflects it. I like my sleep and my schedule reflects it. I like my job and my family reflects it. I like my choice of free time and my lack of relaxation reflects it. I like feeling in control of various aspects of my life and my frustration reflects it. So…since my plans are not the best, I've voted for God to handle my life. He seems to do a better job of it.

I can't explain it, I can't foresee it, and I'm just going to let God do it, and man, does it feel good.

FINAL THOUGHT

Bathroom Jesus is something that we can all have, do have, or will have at some time in our lives. He will grab ahold of us, He will get our attention, and He will have His plans met.

You are part of the plan because you exist. He created you before you entered this earth. You were chosen for this journey because you have a purpose. You were in existence before you were in a body that you are in today.

Psalm 139:15-17

My frame was not hidden from you
when I was made in the secret place,
when I was woven together in the depths of the earth.
Your eyes saw my unformed body;
all the days ordained for me were written in your book
before one of them came to be.
How precious to me are your thoughts, God!
How vast is the sum of them!

You and I were an entity before we were a person. We were souls without human form before the Lord knitted us together with intentional creativity.

Psalm 139:13

For you created my inmost being;
you knit me together in my mother's womb.

You were chosen for this journey. You were chosen for this time of life. You were chosen for this battle. You were chosen to represent the very King of Kings that placed you here. You have a purpose. That purpose, should you choose the mission, is ultimately going to glorify the Lord. How do you accept the mission? Lean into Jesus. Sit with the Lord. Make Him a priority in your life. Make time for Him. Let the model of Jesus be your example. Let the love inside of you shine outward and to God be the glory.

So, when bathroom Jesus shows up, even if it's in your car, you have a decision to make. Either you accept that the Lord wants you to pay attention to something, the Lord wants to spend time with you and invite you into your purpose, the Lord wants you to know that you are remembered, seen and loved, or perhaps all of the above.

No matter how small, no matter how quickly, no matter how vague the experience of knowing, sensing, or interacting with Jesus might be, do not rob yourself of that experience by excusing it away or allowing pride to get in between. Do not surrender the loving connection the Lord is offering to the lame excuses of the enemy. No matter what is going on, or where we are in our journey, the Father can reach us at any time, and He never leaves us. It's us that turns Him away.

(Knock sound on the door) "Who is it?" she asks.

"It's the Way, the Truth, and the Light," is the answer that comes from the other side.

"Um, well...I'm busy. I've had a stressful week and I'm trying to wash all the filth of the day off of me. I just want some peace. You probably shouldn't come in. I'm not in the mood," she answers.

Jesus replies, "I am the Prince of Peace. If you're willing to let me in, I can offer you peace, the filth falls off, and rest will come. But first, you must invite me in."

Only the sound of the running shower broke the stillness of the awkward silence. With a head hung in exhaustion and defeat from the weight of the world, two simple words change everything.

After a long silence, she swallows her pride and makes a decision. "Come in."

BATHROOM JESUS IS REAL WORKBOOK EXPOSED

In Genesis 3:7-11, God asks Adam and Eve where they were. Not because God didn't know they had strayed, but because:

1. He wanted Adam and Eve to be willing to come to Him freely and with repentance.

2. He wanted them to realize that they had chosen to fall into the temptation of the enemy.

3. That they chose something (or someone else) over the promises and relationship with God.

When we look at this today, we might believe that we would have handled things differently, but the reality is we make one or more of these same mistakes every day.

Have you ever felt that you wanted to go to God with something and say you're sorry, but you don't (or didn't) feel like you could?

Yes   or   No

⇒ Was it because of shame? Pain? Pride? The pathway felt blocked because of teachings from religious authorities? OR was it something else you were experiencing? Maybe you didn't know how?

What kept you from going to God with heartfelt apologies, repentance, or sorrow?

_____

_____

_____

What was the circumstance, choice or situation that you felt you needed to go to Him about?

_____

_____

_____

Looking back (if you are beyond that moment) what would you do differently?

_____

_____

_____

Would you like to unburden yourself of this now?

Yes   or   No

If YES, then let's address that now:

Take a moment to relax your body, your shoulders, your neck, and your jaw. Take a deep breath and blow it out. Do it again…

Now, let's chat this out. If you like, follow my lead…

Father, Jesus, God (whatever you call Him), I screwed up. I was dealing with _____ and feeling _____. I just need your help. I messed up. I'm sorry for _____. I need you and your help. I need your guidance.

In the future, how will I know that you are there? --- If something pops into your mind, immediately write it down. Do not discount it. Just write it down.

Use your imagination to picture whatever that burden was that you were holding onto. Was it lying? Cheating? Stealing? Abuse? Betrayal? Anger? Imagine what that looks like as that very burden sits in front of the cross…Take another deep breath and release it into the cross.

Once you do that, let it go. Trust that God heard it and took that burden for you. It's over.

If the answer is NO or you are UNSURE, take a moment to determine why you cannot or do not want to unburden yourself.

Fear?

It's over?

Don't want to go back there?

Just want it to be over?

Take a moment to consider why you answered the way you did and write it down.

_____

_____

_____

God is patient. God is kind. When you are ready…release.

We often wonder "Did God see that?" Or think, "I hope God didn't see that." Or rationalize, "Well, I'm human, so God will forgive that."

You can be sure God did see it, but He's not interested in throwing lightning bolts at you. He's more interested in your awareness and connection with Him. Have you ever pushed the feeling of conviction away? Pushed away the guilt of what you were doing while you were doing it? Did something that you knew was wrong while you were doing it but did it because you were expected to?

Yes or No

If YES, how did you feel while doing that?

_____

_____

_____

Where do you think that conviction, guilt, or knowing of a wrongdoing was coming from at the time?

_____

_____

_____

You see, God put His "laws", His direction, and His moral compass in our minds and on our hearts so He would be in connection with us. As an added awareness to His connection with us, we were granted the Holy Spirit as our helper and our guide.

John 15:26-27 (CSB)

26 "When the Counselor comes, the one I will send to you from the Father —the Spirit of truth who proceeds from the Father—he will testify about me. 27 You also will testify, because you have been with me from the beginning

Looking back, what would you have done differently?

_____

_____

_____

What do you think God was trying to tell you in those moments?

_____

_____

_____

Do you feel like God has forgiven you?

Yes   or   No

Have you forgiven yourself…truly?   Yes   or   No

Here's one we have all dealt with…Think about a moment when you rejected the time you felt God wanted with you.

_____

_____

_____

What was more important for you to fill that time with?

_____

_____

_____

Would you choose the same way now? Why or why not?

_____

_____

_____

What would you do differently today if Jesus or the Holy Spirit alerted you to God's desire to chat and spend time with you?

_____

_____

What if you are at school?

What if you are at work?

What if you are driving?

What if you are out with friends?

What if you are in the middle of doing something that God would not approve of?

Having a plan of action or at least some mental preparation is key to responding in a way that will bring you closer to your goal of doing what both glorifies God and strengthens your relationship with Him. So, take a moment and consider the answers to the above question.

If the King of Kings is trying to get your attention during any of the above, what would be the most reasonable way for you to respond?

_____

_____

_____

Are you prepared to respond that way?

Yes   or   No

Booze, Sex, and Drugs

Yep, we have all been there on some level. Drinking, temptation to drink, expectations to drink…these are very real things. It's how we respond to what God is leading us to do, to know, and to be that matters.

Sex, lust, and wondering thoughts have been made "normal" and acceptable by today's society, but here's the thing…Again, it's how we respond, react and the choices we make versus our interest level in knowing and adhering to what God wants for us every step of the way.

Prescription abuse, opioids, uppers, injection, snorting, edibles, and other intakes of mind-altering influences are choices to numb, avoid, reject, hide from, or shirk back from life. But here's the thing…it CAN also place a wall, a barrier, or dull the senses between ourselves and God. God doesn't hate us when we try and numb out the world, but it does also have a tendency to numb us from God. You see, God never leaves us, but often we turn away from Him so we can deal with our issues, pain, or decisions our way. We run…but just like in the garden, God wants to call us to Him and ask us where we are…He's reaching for us. Even in our messes.

God is reaching out to all of His children at all times. And <u>YES</u>, if you are reading this, missing Him, wanting Him, or praying for HIM, you are one of His children. Do not doubt that! It's a gift that no one should relinquish to anyone. It's yours.

So, take a moment…

Do you recall a time, or a moment when you were tempted or engaged in sex, drugs, or alcohol that you just felt His presence? If so, what was it like?

_____

_____

_____

_____

_____

How did you respond?

_____

_____

_____

Have you talked to God about it since then?

Yes   or   No

Would you like to?   Yes   or   No

If the answer is yes, take a moment to ask Him what He wanted to show you, convey to you, or display to you in that moment. (Write down the very first thing that pops into your head. Don't try to figure it out.)

If the answer is NO or you are UNSURE, take a moment to determine why you cannot or do not want to unburden yourself.

>Fear?

>It's over?

>Don't want to go back there?

>Just want it to be over?

Take a moment to consider why you answered the way you did and write it down.

_____

_____

_____

God is patient and God is kind. When you are ready...release.

Mixed Up with the Wrong Person

Is there someone in your life that you know the Lord has been trying to get you away from? Maybe you're not sure God wants you to get away from them, but you don't feel good in the relationship. Maybe you have some personal conviction or thoughts about how you really don't want to do what they want to do or that they are always focused on their own agenda. Or perhaps you are with someone or know someone who injures you or others emotionally, physically, or mentally only to apologize and do it again? Someone who always has excuses for treating you badly because of jealousy, envy, or because they are leading you into places that do not glorify God?

Take a moment and think it through…If God wants you to get away from them, why do you think that is?

Could it be that you are unequally yoked? Could it be that they are full of pride, or a hardened heart and they want to lead you down that same path? What do you think is going on with God trying to get you away from them?

_____

_____

_____

Why do you think you are resisting?

_____

_____

_____

What do you think God wants you to discover about it today?

_____

_____

_____

Entitlement

I'm going to just say it…We can behave like entitled brats. We have a tendency to pray on Sunday but act like brats when the service concludes and then blame God when we have gone rogue. Here's the thing…God is God all the time. We are human all the time, but what God wants in our humanness is humility, intentionality, and patience. Humility to listen when He's trying to convey something, a choice to be intentional about listening to the conscience, the sensations He conveys, the unctions of the Holy Spirit, and the knowledge that He lays into us. This all requires the patience to move in the spirit when and how He tells us to, not when we "think" or when religion tells us to. God owns all things, including the church and every living creature or creation. So, if anyone knows best, it's Him. That includes connection.

When we choose to let God have some input in our connection with Him, rather than limiting ourselves to a one-way prayer that sounds, feels, and looks more like a monologue, then life changes dramatically.

Take a moment to think back…

When have you blamed God for not being there for you when in truth perhaps you were just not paying attention? Have you ever blamed God for decisions that you made that you think he should have stopped you from making? Give examples.

_____

_____

_____

Rape and Abuse

This is not in the book. However, as a survivor of rape and abuse, I want to address this one separately.

There are times when we have suffered abuse at the hands of others. These were not choices that we made. Instead, they were actions and choices of others forced upon us. More times than I can count I have ministered to women (and some men) that wondered where God was when they were being hurt by the hands of another. Here's the truth…He was there.

He was crying with you. He was grieving with you. He was keeping you sane when your mind was racing. He was sustaining your life so it would not be taken. He was there.

But when we are in survival mode, we don't always think to look for Him in those moments. We don't have the wherewithal to even consider He was sustaining us, covering us, or grieving with us. The truth is we often get angry because He didn't stop it for us.

But listen to me…He never left you. You were not alone. There will be or is a testimony of how He pulled you through it. How He protected you from worse. How He changed the trajectory of what could have been to something less. God wastes nothing in our lives. You are stronger, wiser, have discernment, and you don't have to fear anything any longer. The enemy cannot take anything from your mind or spirit except what you choose to give away.

If you have anger…Choose to release. Not for the predator, but because releasing them means releasing yourself. Choose to live and not just survive. It's a far better road.

SEX & SIN

This is an unpopular topic, but here are some truths that you will not hear in many churches.

Sex and sin are an issue because during sex there is a spiritual exchange. Yep, I said it…Sex isn't just risky because of STDs and viruses, but for good or bad, there is a spiritual exchange. Who we have sex with is who we are linked with. We become one…

I'm not making this up.

1 Corinthians 6:15-17 (CSB)

"Don't you know that your bodies are a part of Christ's body? So should I take a part of Christ's body and make it part of a prostitute? Absolutely not! Don't you know that anyone joined to a prostitute is one body with her? For Scripture says, The two will become one flesh. But anyone joined to the Lord is one spirit with him."

Take a moment and think back…How many people have you broken spiritual boundaries with? What of yours did you give away and what of theirs did you inherit? Maybe you know or maybe you don't, but there is a way to correct the issue.

1. Stop…Make a decision that you are going to protect all that God gave you and reject what others may have.

2. Reinforce that boundary with a choice not to proceed with sexual contact.

3. Ask the Lord to remove any unholy soul ties or spiritual impurities that you have in place as a result of that relationship(s).

4. Ask the Lord to give you back the parts of you that you gave away.

5. Make a choice to move forward without looking back in self condemnation but instead forward with a new understanding.

Look at number one. Are you truly willing to stop and make a decision to stop? Be honest with yourself.

Yes   or   No

If YES, regarding number two, are you willing to express to your partner that you are not returning to former behaviors?

Yes   or   No

Are you afraid of losing them if you tell them of your choice?

Yes   or   No

(If someone loves you with any depth, the sex is not going to matter. Sex is designed to nurture a relationship that is ordained by God. It was not designed as a source of recreation. If the relationship is ordained by God, then God will sustain it with hearts that are willing and reflect His heart.)

Move on to number three…

Take a moment to sit quietly and ask the Lord to reveal to you soul ties and impurities. Write them down as they are revealed. If you don't feel, sense, or receive anything in your spirit that tells you what you want removed, then ask Him to just remove what you are not able to know. Are you willing to do that?

If so, write what He reveals here:

Soul ties:

_____

_____

Impurities:

_____

_____

Moving on to number four, ask Him to reveal to you what it is that you have given away. This applies to both males and females. Write down what you feel, sense, know, or receive in your spirit.

I gave away:

_____

_____

If you don't receive any understanding of what you gave away, ask Him to just correct it.

And number five…choose not to look back.

DRUGS & ALCOHOL

Here's how powerful and sovereign God is. More than one person has told stories of meeting Him in the lowest points of their lives, totally out of their heads and under influences.

Were those encounters real…probably. Do we discount them because of their state of mind? Yes, but God reaches His children, and He keeps reaching until we are ready to reach up to Him and ask Him to save us from ourselves.

When reading the chapter on drugs and alcohol, did anything remind you of any circumstances that you might have been in during your life? Or perhaps you have heard of someone having an experience like that? What does that teach you about who God truly is?

What character trait of God do you see in this desire to reach us when we choose so badly?

_____

_____

How do you think it applies to that circumstance?

_____

_____

If you spend some time thinking about and can't connect any character traits, then it's important that you get to know your heavenly Father a bit better. Until then, here are a few that might apply:

Love, Mercy, Grace, Patience, Kindness, Gentleness, Loyalty, Protective

BUSYNESS & CONTROL

When reading the Busyness chapter, did you consider what occupies so much of your time? Is the majority of time spent on or with a particular subject or person? Are you preoccupied with something that takes up brain space? Something that keeps you up or your mind swimming? Is your schedule so tight that there's not much room or time for thoughts, praise, worship, or interaction with the Lord?

What are three things you can do in your life today that will free up half an hour a day for meditating on Him, reading about Him, praising Him, or worshiping Him that you are NOT currently doing now.

1. _____
2. _____
3. _____

For those who listen to worship music in their vehicles already, how can you add half an hour of one or the other elements of connection? Reading the scriptures, meditating on Him, praise, prayer, asking questions?

_____

_____

Sometimes there is a control issue that needs to be addressed. We forget that we exist because He chose us. We forget that we are alive because we have a part in this journey that He gifted us with. We forget that we were assigned a purpose, one that we were each uniquely destined for. We didn't have any input into any of that. Those were all loving gifts. However, we often use that very statement as a reason to push back on God. "I didn't choose to be here."

In our own little versions of rebellion for being handpicked by the King of the universe, we try and control the journey, direction, timing, and outcomes. With that comes the pushback of flesh when dealing with our relationship with God.

Take a moment to think about what you have heard or even said over your lifetime about making time for connection with God.

What are the general excuses people, or perhaps you, use for not making time for God? How many can you come up with?

1. _____
2. _____
3. _____
4. _____

5. _____

6. _____

7. _____

8. _____

9. _____

10. _____

How many of those have you used? _____

Do you feel that they are real reasons for not taking time or are they just mental blocks or resistance to change? Or something else?

_____

_____

What are you willing to change to lean closer to God?

_____

_____

THE REAL DEAL

We all know how to behave when we are faced with a religious circumstance. Posture, hands folded, speak quietly, make sure you use proper Christian responses when responding to people, smile, and don't forget to tithe.

Meanwhile…Your hands are sweating from nerves or emotion, your mind is wandering, you want to say something that you stop on your tongue before it gets out of your mouth, you feel like you should be there or you don't want to be there and your smile is so fake you know other people might see it so you work harder to make it look real.

Let's get real….

What do you want to say about God, to God, or speak out about regarding your relationship with God that you can't say or don't feel like you can say?

_____
_____
_____
_____
_____
_____

Do you believe:

Once I say it, people will look at me differently?

Once I say it, God will be mad at me?

Once I say it, I will be condemned?

Once I say it, people will see me differently or learn who I truly am?

I don't want to admit the way I feel?

What do you believe about saying how you feel?

_____

_____

Take a moment to ask yourself why you feel what you feel about God's responses. About the response of people. About where these beliefs came from and about how they impact you.

This is an opportunity for growth. God knows you, accepts you, and loves you. It's time you know yourself.

What is at least one thing that you feel you learned from this book that changes, reinforces, or validates your mindset, concept, understanding, or conversation with God?

1. _____
2. _____
3. _____
4. _____
5. _____
6. _____
7. _____

There are so many aspects of our lives that we have adopted from others. There are many worldviews of others that have been conveyed to us that have altered our perspectives. There are many things that have been spoken over us, to us, and about us that we have absorbed as truths. Sometimes, we learn to adhere to the definitions assigned to us by others.

It's important that we take a moment to learn why we believe what we believe.

Why we do what we do.

Why we feel what we feel.

And most importantly how we respond to that inner longing we have for something bigger, something supernatural, something that we know deep inside is calling to us.

Bathroom Jesus is real, He chases us down because He will only let us wander so far. He's a good Father.

    God Bless

www.ingramcontent.com/pod-product-compliance
Lightning Source LLC
Chambersburg PA
CBHW060402080526
44583CB00012B/440